# My New Family

## CHRISTINA KELLY

ISBN 979-8-88644-553-4 (Paperback)
ISBN 979-8-88644-554-1 (Digital)



Covenant Books
11661 Hwy 707
Murrells Inlet, SC 29576
www.covenantbooks.com

To my husband, Kevin Leroy.
For always encouraging my imagination
and supporting my dreams.
Look at us now!

To my children Amanda Diann and Ryan Creed.
Never grow up so much you forget to
see things colorful and fun.
Dreams do come true.

"Today is the day! Today is the day!" Lou Lou yelled.

"What's all the fuss about?" Oliver asked.

"We are getting adopted today, silly," Lou Lou explained.

"I am so excited to get to meet our new family! I wonder what they will be like," Oliver said.

"Could they live in a castle with a moat surrounding us with green, green, grass as far as the eye can see, or maybe they live in a cottage deep in the forest with furry friends, or maybe they live by the ocean where mermaids visit us every day."

"Or maybe they live in a regular home just like Papa does now," Oliver replied with a snap. "Come on, Lou Lou, get your head out of the clouds. Here comes Papa with our breakfast. It's going to be a long day."

During breakfast, we heard new voices coming toward us. It must be our new family.

Could that be... It is!

"Look, Oliver, they are here," Lou Lou replied.

"You've been a little grouchy since Papa told us the news. Don't be grouchy about meeting our new family and moving to a new home. It's all going to be okay. We must make a good impression today."

"I am not worried one bit. It is an adventure. And I am excited," said Lou Lou.

Lou Lou was watching with anticipation.

"Oh, look! That lady is coming closer to us, Oliver. It must be her, it's our new mom. Look at her long, beautiful hair. She is beautiful. Her voice, it's so soft. Almost a whisper."

I love my new mom already; she is so gentle with Oliver and me. Her voice and smile are comforting.

"I think this is going to be a perfect fit. Don't you, Oliver?"

"At least we will be together," Oliver says.

Our new mom picked us up one at a time and... *Wait*, why are they putting us in this box? It is dark in here. It is scary in here. *Hello!* What's happening?

Okay, Lou Lou, don't freak out. Be brave. You've got to be brave for Oliver. You both can't freak out. Oh, I am freaking out. I am feeling woozy. Ugh, Mom. What are you thinking, Lou Lou? She can't hear you?

"Oliver, this will be a great time for a nap. Don't you think so? I mean, it's dark after all. And maybe if we sleep, we won't get carsick, and the trip will be over before we know it," Lou Lou replied.

"I'm not worried," Oliver replied. "Now go on to sleep, Lou Lou. You ramble when you're excited."

Moments later, "How much longer, I wonder?" Oliver spoke out loud.

Lou Lou wakes up. "I can't sleep with all these bumps and weird noises."

"Sorry to wake you. It seemed like you were having a nice dream. But I am bored. This trip has got to be over soon."

"I did have a nice dream," Lou Lou replied. "I dreamed we were at a big, nice home, sitting in the middle of a pasture with grazing grass as far as we could see and a deep valley with a stream that ran through. We were making all kinds of new friends that looked different than us. There were frogs, snails, fish, birds, lizards, snakes..." Lou Lou said."

"I get the picture," Oliver replied with a grumble.

"Well, it was nice, and we had lots of friends, and I was having fun playing." Lou Lou snapped back at Oliver.

"Oliver," Lou Lou said.

"Listen, I think we are here. We have finally stopped."

"I can't believe we arrived!" Lou Lou said with excitement.

Wait, we are moving. Ugh! I think I am going to be carsick again.

"No, wait. Mom is getting us out of the car. We are home. We made it, Oliver."

Mom gently opened the box and picked us up. She carried us around to show us our new home and gently set us down after a long day's ride at what appeared to be...

"The best living space *ever!*" Lou Lou shouted. "It is a little different, but I think I will like it just fine. It is nice and warm here. Don't you think so, Oliver?"

Oliver looked at how Momma was making sure we were getting settled and comfortable. "Yes," Oliver replied, "I think we will be happy here."

"I knew we had nothing to worry about," Lou Lou said, with a gleam in her eyes.

I love my new home. It's warm and cozy.

I think our new family is a perfect fit. They have thought of everything to make us feel right at home.

Yay! Look! There is Momma again. I hope she is bringing food. I am hungry.

Nope. She is bringing a bunch of people to us; I think she is showing us off to her friends.

Like any proud momma would.

*Hey, did any of you smiling faces bring food?* Lou Lou pondered, staring up at all the people.

*Ah! What is that smell?*

"Woohoo, Oliver, it is time to eat. Food! Moving day really made us work up an appetite. Come on, Oliver, let's eat.

Lou Lou yawns. "It's been a long day. It must be getting close to bedtime, or maybe I ate too much. Oliver, I am sleepy. What a day. Everyone wanting to touch us and tell us how cute we are is tiring."

"Good night," Oliver told Lou Lou. "I'm beat."

"We can't go to bed, Oliver. Momma still has her friends here."

"It looks like they are starting to leave."

Finally, Momma *is telling everyone bye. Maybe it is* bedtime, Lou Lou thought

This has been the best day ever.

Oh, look, she is making her way back over to us. She's turning the lights down. Perfect timing, Momma. She knows us already.

"Good night, Oliver. Good night, Lou Lou," Momma said.
See you tomorrow.
Good night, Momma.

# About the Author

Christina was born and raised in Texas and always had an abundance of animals to grow up with. The phrase "Once upon a time" is how she lives her life, so books are an essential part of her life. She and her husband even owned a small-town bookstore at one point in their lives. With her love of animals and books, it was only a matter of time before the two merged into reality for her.

She was inspired to write her story about one of her familiar loves, tortoises. She had the privilege of raising two sulcata tortoises from the time they were babies to adulthood. This book is about sharing adventures through the tortoise's eyes. Bringing to life how fun they were to own while also sharing how they, too, have their own personalities.